MELISSA MOLOMO

Everything you need to know that
they should of taught you.

This book is dedicated to those who seek to
be better than they were yesterday.
I hope you take all that soothes you.

DEAR READER,

It is my dream for this book to inspire humanity toward greatness—for the more kindhearted we have in the world, the less people will desire to be evil.

Love,

Melissa Molomo
"Ms. Say What's Real"

Each and every single one of us has endless potential, but we don't always use it to our fullest advantage. You chose to read this book, so I already know you have a **desire to be great**. You seek to better yourself, and you are always looking to take the next step.

Well, first things first: we can all start by no longer settling in our lives. There is always room for improvement, especially self-improvement.

Acknowledge the fact that **your worth is endless.**

We cannot keep allowing **FEAR** to stand its ground, nor give anyone the power to say we're not good enough. We shouldn't stand by idly and prove them right by not doing anything about it. We have to put our foot down for what is right. **We MUST fight.**

When I say fight, I don't mean physically. I mean mentally fight the demons that manifest within our individual insecurities. Distance yourself from the people who are telling you that your dreams are too big for reality. *Stop anyone and anything from planting seeds into your brain telling you, "You can't do this,"* *because you know what? YOU CAN!* I'm not just speaking motivationally here—this is the flat-out truth. ☺

EACH AND EVERY ONE OF US HAS WHAT IT TAKES TO BE GREAT.

It's just those who have the audacity to be so, do so. It's up to you to take your reason and run wild with it. Who cares if people look at you as if you're crazy? They're going to do that regardless. Do you have any idea how many people came to me and didn't fully understand what I was trying to do, and tried to discourage me, telling me it wasn't possible? Well, here you are reading my book. Hence, anything is possible.

You, my friend, are a masterpiece as is. So let me tell you something that I will tell to my future children: "If someone tries to dim your light, it's only because they don't understand your brightness and don't see things the way you do—do not fret and do not let them shade you. **Keep shining because if someone doesn't notice your potential, they will never fully realize your worth.**"
Therefore, this isn't somebody you should want on your team anyway. If they decide to change sides and root for you then let them root for you, but this time around from the sidelines.

And as for me… *I'm already rooting for you.*

HELLO,

I AM A DREAM CHASER.
I WILL NOT STOP RUNNING
UNTIL I CATCH MY DREAMS.

I AM DEDICATED 100%
BLOOD - SWEAT – TEARS
EVERYTHING I'VE GOT
EVERYDAY.

I STRIVE TO SUCCEED.
I DESIRE TO BE GREAT.
I LIVE TO BECOME
LEGENDARY.

I WILL NOT GIVE UP.
SO WHO'S GOING TO STOP ME?
WHO'S TO TELL ME I CAN'T?

THE ANSWER IS NO ONE.

IN ORDER TO BE GREAT, ONE MUST BE WILLING TO BE CRITICIZED.

This does not mean you have to listen to all of it. That's the power of "in one ear and out the other." Just be aware that criticism is always there. Due to social media, it's not only the magazines and tabloids being critics anymore. Nevertheless, you can still block out the hate. If I were famous, I'd probably hire someone to do that. It's one thing to share your opinion to help enlighten someone, but if you're just trying to break someone down with your careless words than that's a whole different ball game. I mean, really, if you don't like somebody why are you even wasting your time bothering with them? That says more about you than them. Someone's definition of you doesn't define who you are; it defines how they perceive things.

We've all witnessed people respond more to hateful remarks and focus their effort on trying to set people straight instead of recognizing and giving credit to the people who actually love them. Focus on the love. Bullying will exist even more when there's a live audience. Close the curtain on them.

No matter who you are and what you do, there is always going to be somebody who doesn't like you, but that's why there's so much power in delete and block buttons.

Use them. Don't drown yourself in harmful words.

7

DROWN THE NEGATIVE...

Stop being angry, disappointed or doing things that you don't want to be doing. You will only end up miserable that way. (Unless it's certain things like cleaning up, paying bills or things that MUST get done...catch my drift?) Time is the most valuable gift that we are given and the way we choose to spend it is most important.

Do not waste your time on mixed emotions and temporary people. If it's not going to matter years from now, try not to waste a chance at being happy and spreading love. You are doing yourself a tremendous favor when you let go of the things that poison you. When there are toxic conversations and attitudes surrounding you, do everything in your power to **take a deep breath and inhale compassion, kindness and love, then exhale hatred, judgments and misunderstandings.** You have much better things to do with your days than to hold a grudge.

PATIENCE...

...now that's f*#king golden.

There is someone out there in the world that doesn't have to be forced to fit into your puzzle. Do not take the risk of settling for someone if you're uncertain of your feelings just because you want some kind of companionship. There is someone out there who is meant for you. Leave the door open for them to come in. Until then: **Focus on you.** Focus on pursuing your goals and give yourself the opportunity to make your dreams come true without being distracted by detours. Surround yourself with family, loyal loved ones and successful people, that way you'll learn how to succeed from them. Learn to better yourself every day by taking what they teach you and teaching what they taught you. Be patient and keep yourself busy. Allow love to catch up to you, but on its own time.

If you aren't having fun and laughing throughout your day, you're doing something terribly wrong.

Your life doesn't have to be so serious. Have fun. Giggle a bit. It's healthy for you.

Seriously. If you don't believe me... Google it.

TAKE YOUR TIME...

Take the time you need to self reflect and not think about everyone and everything that's going on around you. Instead of clogging your thoughts with poison, focus on cleansing the brain by finding complete contentment and happiness within thyself.

Listen to soothing music.
Sit by the beach.
Exercise.
Meditate.
Write / Draw.

Do whatever it takes to bring out your inner peace.

Focus on your breathing:
Inhale.
Exhale.
Take deep breaths.

And at the end of this process, pat yourself on the back and give yourself some credit for taking the time to love and heal yourself. It's well deserved at this point.

10

DO NOT SETTLE:

Do not settle for someone who isn't willing to fight for you.

Do not settle for someone who has messed up in the past and doesn't care enough to make things right in the present.

Do not settle for someone who only tries when it's convenient for them.

Do not settle for someone who shows no progress when progression seriously needs to be shown.

Do not settle for lies and manipulation.

Do not settle for things you do not deserve such as disrespect, betrayal and abuse.

Do not settle for basic, baby. Extraordinary is where it's at.

Once you start to settle, you start to accept and the only thing you are doing is driving yourself crazy.

YOU ARE UNIQUE. YOU ARE BEAUTIFUL. AND YOU ARE LOVED.
You are worth way more than you can imagine.
Somewhere, somebody is waiting for someone like you every day.

Today could be the day. ***DO NOT LOSE HOPE.***

11

Melissa Molomo

When you lose motivation and hope, getting yourself out of that funk seems borderline impossible. Sometimes it takes that ONE person to give you the extra push you've been waiting for, but at the end of the day always remember the only person who can make you fail in life is YOU.

Hip-hop producer and rapper Chase N Cashe told me, "Life is messed up and if you're not a warrior and don't make a shield and a sword out of something, then you will get eaten alive." His words sparked a wildfire within me that not even 100 hoses could put out, or make me believe what I want in life cannot happen. I knew all along I was going to be successful, but procrastination can be an issue. Even when people doubted me, I never once doubted myself. If I could tell you anything, I'd tell you to prepare to fight for your dreams, your goals, and your loved ones because anything worth having in life will not come or stay easily. Too many people in this life are going to tell you things you can't do. So many people are going to purposely test you because they want to see you fail. They want to see if you have what it takes to succeed in life. *You have to want it badly enough to the point where no matter how many times you've been knocked down, you confidently get back up and say "I can do this."*

To everyone who has doubted you throughout the years, to everyone who has given you a chance and has taken it away from you, and to everyone who has stolen your spotlight— you make sure to PROVE THEM ALL WRONG...not in a way of spite, but in a way of light. *Turn your doubters into believers...* Trip, fall and hit rock bottom for all anyone cares. As long as you get back up and succeed against all odds— **You are the true definition of a warrior.**

13

WHAT YOU PUT INTO THE UNIVERSE CAN COME BACK TO YOU TENFOLD WHEN YOU LEAST EXPECT IT. EVEN THE SMALLEST THOUGHT HAS POWER. INCLUDING THE DREAMS THAT YOU HAVE. THINK GOOD THOUGHTS AND SPREAD POSITIVE ENERGY. DON'T COMPARE OR COMPETE. SHOW COMPASSION AND KINDNESS. DON'T POINT FINGERS. LEARN TO LOVE UNCONDITIONALLY. DON'T BEND TO BREAK. HEAL AND BUILD.

WHAT YOU THINK AND WHAT YOU DO SHOULD ALWAYS BE IN HARMONY.

FOR MY SINGLES:
(Read this aloud)

I am strong.
I am independent.
I do not need a spouse to make me whole; although it would be nice to grow old with somebody.
I am completely content being alone right now because I know who I am.
I know I have one of the strongest loves a human being can offer.
I will not settle for anything temporary.
I deserve loyalty.
I deserve respect.
I deserve authentic love.
I will not choose to settle until I get what I fully deserve.
My heart is more than silver or gold, and my worth is something that most cannot easily afford, especially when it comes to morals.
We've learned to rush, but not to wait.
I will wait, and
I will continue on this journey independently, loving me.

And when I finally bump into you for taking the same path—I will ask you in a jokingly, but serious manner..."What the hell took you so long?"

THE KEY TO HAPPINESS IS STAYING AWAY FROM THE PEOPLE WHO CONSISTENTLY HURT YOU.

Our generation is filled with so much temptation, dishonesty and false advertising due to social networks and technological devices. It almost seems that chivalry is dead because instead of getting a knock on the door, you get a text stating, "I'm here." Well, here's an FYI… **Chivalry is not dead and neither are morals.** Want to know how I know…because there are people in this world just like you and me. The person you are drawn to just might not have what it takes to offer it to you. There are so many options all at the click of a button that people are no longer satisfied; what they are seeing is too appealing to the eye causing them to not think much about doing right by one another, because their wants for that moment become more important than their needs.

I want you to know there are good people out there. When you find them, hopefully you will end up appreciating them more because you'll realize they're a rarity. When you have them, hold onto them. Pay them back with loyalty, love and truth at all times because too many people are looking for the next best thing, instead of being content with what they already have. Not even knowing that it's better than good enough.

Love is being real and being loyal even when you're mad and tempted not to be.

What you are attracted to could be what's messing you up. So, you've made a few bad choices when it comes to love. We all have. If you're not happy, try to change your "type" a little bit in order to receive a different result.

NO MATTER HOW BEAUTIFUL YOU ARE, HAVING A ROTTEN PERSONALITY MAKES YOU LOOK UGLY.

~~FRI~~ENDSHIPS...

One thing I wish I had learned in high school was that most of your "friends" would be temporary and not long term. They're seasonal. Here I go getting myself into trouble for people who I thought were my real friends, but little did I know...

Friendship is not a popularity contest. It's not about how many people you think you know or how well known you may be. If you end up having one TRUE friend that you can count on that's more than enough to last a lifetime.

Even social media has us all convinced of false friendships. Friendship isn't a matter of "LIKES" and "COMMENTS." It's about the people who are actually there for you and care for you in real life. They're the ones you should cherish.

So when you're out and about, put your phone down and live in the moment!

WOMEN EMPOWERMENT:

Women really should start working together instead of constantly going against one another. We should have respect for ourselves and each other at all times. Even if a woman happens to be a complete stranger—treat that woman, as you would want to be treated. We need to stop bashing one another and start building each other up. If only all women would take the time to understand this, men could no longer use this very thing against us to divert the attention away from them. Insecurities, betrayal and cheating would no longer exist if we had each other's backs. Start today. Be honest. Be selfless. Be kind. Stop making these women your enemies and start showing them the empowerment of sisterhood.

"When women come together with a collective intention, magic happens."
- Phylicia Rashad

19

THE MAIN REASON WHY PEOPLE ARE DOING BADLY IS BECAUSE THEY SURROUND THEMSELVES WITH PEOPLE WHO HAVE LOW SELF-ESTEEM.

If you want to do something with your life surround yourself with the winners, the different ones, the ones who don't take "no" for an answer, the crazy creative ones who aren't afraid to admit it, the hustlers, the go-getters, the ones who've been repeatedly knocked down, but still have enough courage to get back up and are ready to rumble. Those are the people you should want to be around. Do you want to be successful? Surround yourself with successful people: you'll learn how to succeed from watching them.

"If you haven't found it yet, keep looking. Don't settle. As with all matters of the heart, you'll know when you find it. And, like any great relationship, it just gets better and better as the years roll on."
-Steve Jobs

LEARN FROM EVERY EXPERIENCE YOU ARE GIVEN!

Gain insight from everyone. Everyone is inspiring in his or her own way. Some set great examples, others happen to show you what not to do. Beware of the people you seek advice from. Not everyone is in it for your best interest. Be selective. Stay around the people who know and care about you the most. Otherwise you're going to surround yourself with people who have ulterior motives who never want to see you doing better than them. Always remember: There is way more out there than what you are feeling right now. Let go of everything that happened to you in the past and give yourself a clean slate. You'll feel better about yourself once you feel brand new. Today is a new beginning. Start fresh.

TURN LONELINESS INTO WHOLENESS...

There is a huge strength in being alone. There is power behind finding 'you', and shaping who you are. Don't worry about what everybody else needs. It's about having the strength to fight off loneliness instead of settling for comfort. We must learn to stand on our own two feet. Choose to learn your own ways first. Find your own path, instead of finding yourself lost on a detour in the middle of someone else's. There is nothing better than stability; what's better than a little peace of mind? Everyone has their own baggage to carry; there is no need to bombard them with yours.

Be proud of your independence and taking the time to fully love and understand yourself. Being alone will make you realize who deserves a chance with what you have to offer. You'll also soon discover who doesn't deserve the time of day. Continue following the path you are given. Don't choose to be misled by the misguided. Be patient enough to know who you are in order to completely understand who somebody else is.

This way, you are allowing someone to come along who will willingly love you for 'you', without the pressure of being molded into someone you wouldn't have chosen to be on your own.

...ALWAYS CHOOSE TO HAVE A HEALTHY RELATIONSHIP WITH YOURSELF BEFORE YOU EVER DECIDE TO HAVE AN UNHEALTHY RELATIONSHIP WITH SOMEONE ELSE.

THE WORDS: "I'M SORRY." USE THEM! JUST DON'T KEEP ASKING FOR FORGIVENESS, IF YOU PLAN ON DOING IT AGAIN.

While we're here... I might as well.

There are some words I wish I had left unsaid. There are some things I wish I never did, but I guess you can say that's all part of the human experience—learning from your mistakes and growing from them. I'm not looking to give you an excuse. I genuinely just want to say I'm sorry to those I've ever hurt along the way. I hope you know that was never my intention.

And if once upon a time it was, I hope you can forgive me.

FOR MY COUPLES:

It is very important to be a safe haven for your mate. After a stressful day at work, dealing with inconsiderate people or even having family issues, your spouse should be that one person who has your back, deals with all your nonsense and drama, through thick and thin—no matter what!

Designate days for each other; set weekly goals. Remember, it isn't about finding the time, but about making the time. Make it all about them. Once they come home from work, whatever they ask, simply do it.

- Give a massage.
- Go for a walk together.
- Watch their choice of movie or television show.
- Treat them to dinner at their favorite restaurant, or cook their favorite meal.
- Have a candlelit bath ready with soothing music playing.

Tonight when they get home talk about this with them. It will help keep the spark alive. One day, have it made all about you, and the next day, make it all about your lover—that way when you come home, stress will be relieved, not caused.

TRAIN YOUR BRAIN!

If you don't like your life, change who you are.

If you don't like the people around you, change your surroundings.

If you don't like your job, find one you like.

There are solutions to every problem. Start fixing them.

Either make a change or make an excuse.

It's your choice.

Thinking about something negative puts negative energy into the universe. You are what you attract. **If you're busy thinking about all the wrong in your life, guess what? Nothing is going to get better!** Not with that attitude. You have to train your brain to think and remain positive even through moments of tragedy. If you keep positive thoughts in your head, you will start to receive positive actions, and if the actions you're receiving aren't always positive at least your reactions are.

Give it time.

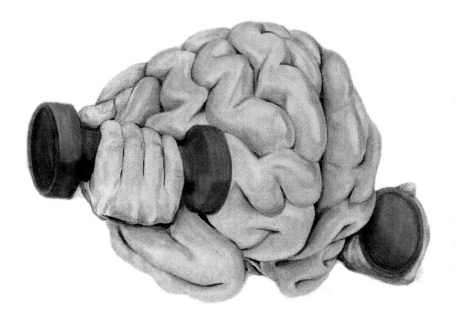

TEMPTATION IS FOR THE WEAK-MINDED.

When two people are in a relationship and you are well aware of that, simply RESPECT it and have enough respect for yourself to not even go there. There are plenty of fish in the sea. *There is no need to try and mess with a fish that's already been caught.*

Be careful, karma does come back around. I'm pretty positive you wouldn't want that done to you, would you? In all honesty, if two people are content with each other, you should never try to sneak your way in to sabotage a good thing.

However, if a spouse has the audacity to play along and feed into weak-minded nonsense due to "something missing in their relationship," then they no longer deserve to be with someone loyal and true to them anyway. If they are going to resort to sneaking around, in the long run it's the cheaters who are always cheating themselves. Bottom line, if you catch yourself wandering in a relationship you might as well get lost.

Melissa Molomo

*"You cannot do a kindness too soon,
for you never know
how soon it will be too late."*
-Ralph Waldo Emerson

T reat everyone with respect and kindness. You might not always get it back, but when you do, it sure is great. Everyone you come across is going through something. If you haven't been, just be a little more aware of this. You're either adding to it or you're serving as an escape for this person.

The people who cause the most harm are those who are suffering themselves; remember that when dealing with them. Be cautious you don't add fuel to the fire. Let us mend those who are broken, instead of being their breaking point.

Imagine a world where there was no such thing as money, and people were given things and got paid based on **real** acts of kindness. If that's how we lived on a day-to-day basis...

A lot of the people would be in big trouble.

STOP DREADING ALL THE BAD STUFF.

It's really not worth it. Your stress isn't going to get you anywhere. Life is too short to be anything less than happy. i'm not trying to bullshit you and say everything is going to be all peaches and cream because it's not. Some days are going to be so bad that you don't even know why you bother, but that's life. You have to roll with the punches. Just as bad days come and go, so do the good— sometimes even amazing—days. Focus on those. Everyone should try to focus on the bigger and better things instead of sweating the small stuff.

Leave it behind. Learn to be happy with yourself, the life you live and the people you choose to be around. Life goes on with or without you, so while you're here, get yourself out of that funk, stop feeling sorry for yourself and leave your mark.

YOU ARE NOT RESPONSIBLE FOR ANYONE'S HAPPINESS BUT YOUR OWN. HOWEVER, YOU CAN CHOOSE TO MAKE OTHER PEOPLE HAPPY WHENEVER YOU'RE AROUND.

FAIRYTALES ONLY EXIST FOR PEOPLE WHO BELIEVE IN THEM ENOUGH TO CREATE THEM.

There is no such thing as a perfect relationship, although it is something that we all seek and crave. It's nearly impossible for two souls to get along perfectly, to confide in one another perfectly, to provide for another perfectly and to love one another perfectly. A relationship is what two souls decide to make out of it, which could be endless.

People only tell and show you what they are comfortable with you knowing. A couple can look picture perfect, but a picture is only worth a thousand words. You'll never know the everyday struggle a couple faces, the misunderstandings they have, and the challenges they face along their journey. Do not discourage them—they are being courageous by risking their hearts for a chance at love, unconditional love. That may not mean perfect, but it's real, and that's all that matters.

In order to have a successful relationship, two people have to be in a relationship where no matter what happens—ups, downs, lefts, rights—you BOTH will do whatever it takes to make it work. When it comes to love, it takes the effort of two people. **It is never single-sided.** Once it becomes single-sided, the relationship will begin to fall apart. If the person you are with is not worth the extra mile in your eyes, then that is someone's time you should no longer waste.

BE SO FOCUSED ON YOUR OWN APPEARANCE THAT YOU'LL LOOK IN THE MIRROR BEFORE YOU EVEN THINK ABOUT JUDGING ANOTHER HUMAN BEING.

You are forgiven and you are loved, but you are not flawless.

You are a sinner. It's okay to make mistakes, just try not to be blinded. Open your eyes. Be wise enough to learn from them and not repeat them.

Better yourself.

The only person you should be in competition with is the person looking back at you in the mirror. Today, be a better image than the person you were yesterday. Tomorrow, be even better than you were today.

WHEN NOTHING SEEMS TO BE
GOING RIGHT IN LIFE, WE
MUST TAKE OURSELVES OUT
OF OUR SHELLS.

TAKE TIME TO HEAL.
STOP BLAMING EVERYONE
AND EVERYTHING FOR THE
RUT WE CONTINUE TO PUT
OURSELVES IN.

DON'T BE DEFENSIVE-ASK
YOURSELF: WHAT AM I DOING
WRONG? WHAT DO I WANT
TO CHANGE?

THE CHANGE BEGINS WITH
YOU. NOW, LET'S GET
STARTED.

A big motivational push for me was my loved ones telling me what's right from wrong, but who's to say what's right from wrong for me?

OPINIONS
ARE
A
BITCH,
ESPECIALLY
FOR
THE
STUBBORN.

I had to prove to them I could get things done MY WAY. Not the highway.

Melissa Molomo

HI, I'M STUBBORN. IT'S NICE TO MEET YOU...

What works for me might not necessarily work for you, and vice versa, but please, do not try to persuade someone, or assume someone is living wrong because they choose to go a different route or live a different lifestyle than the way you do. Everyone is different; even though we all have similar emotions, we may not all feel and operate the same. I can be successful sleeping a little late and working all night long until sunrise, while you can be successful working 9-5, 5 days a week. It's whatever works best for YOU. Success depends not only on the person with great ideas, but those who believe in themselves enough to not give up. Successful people devote their time, effort and talent into their passions with careful execution.

If someone is determined, let's not discourage. The world needs more encouragers. We should respect each other's visions, because everybody has a different perspective.

The way you think and operate may not be the same as someone else. Respect their vision and focus on yours. We don't build our dreams by breaking theirs.

> "Never interrupt someone doing what you said couldn't be done."
> -Amelia Earhart

35

BE GRATEFUL FOR YOUR BROKEN HEART AND FOR ALL THE TIMES YOU WERE LIED TO. BOTH ONLY LED YOU TO APPRECIATE THE TRUTH AND CHERISH PEOPLE WITH MORALS.

SUPERWOMAN:

"I was never raised to replace a man. I was raised to become more of a woman."

My father decided to leave me when I was 4 years old, which left my mother alone with 4 children—no income, no home, absolutely nothing. She had to start from scratch. My mother clearly hit rock bottom. She lost the only person she had revered as the love of her life, talk about the ultimate betrayal. Not only did she lose her husband, but she also lost the person who she believed would be an amazing father to her children.

She had two choices: 1. Give up, or 2. Hit the ON switch into survival mode; which do you think she chose? My mother worked 3 jobs, went to church for food and clothing and even relied on certain family members to help with other things. My Uncle Ralph assumed the father figure role in my life as much as possible. I remember how he used to take extra care in making sure I felt loved—along with my three older brothers, as men of the house: Michael, Nicholas and Anthony. The house that we lost due to my father's actions—my mother actually bought back for us 3 years later on her own. It is the very house we live in now, thanks to all of her hard work. She did what she had to as a Mother for our family to survive. She has and will always be my inspiration.

At 24 years old, I am sitting here, typing this in the living room of my HOME that she bought back for us! I am still in awe that my mother did this for us. Not to mention, not once did my mother bring a man into this home as a replacement for my father, no matter what happened between the two of them. She put all of her love, energy and devotion into her children when in all reality she didn't have to. My mother became more of a woman doing what she had to do instead of waiting and relying on a man to get it done for her. For such a tragic time in her life, she showed herself no mercy and made it so beautiful for us. Who would have thought the real life superwoman… is my mother.

Mom,

If you're reading this, which I know you are because you are my biggest supporter, I admire you. You sacrificed your whole entire life for us, and anyone who is blinded towards your greatness, I feel sorry for them. You are the most amazing, selfless, beautiful human being on planet earth, with a heart made out of gold. Words couldn't express my gratitude. I am forever indebted to you for what you've done. I thank you with every single piece of my heart for not giving up on us. You could have, but you didn't. So for that I will forever treasure you. You are the best mother and father a daughter could have. I pray I can take care of you one day like you have done for my brothers and I all these years. Have no worries. Get rid of all of your fears. Everything is going to be okay. I have you and you have me. You are my Queen, my angel, my best friend and greatest of all—my mother.

I LOVE YOU MOMMY!

IF WE ALWAYS HAVE OUR GUARDS UP AND ARE SO AFRAID OF TAKING CHANCES, WE LOSE THE OPPORTUNITIES THAT COULD LEAD TO OUR SUCCESS.

DO NOT LET FEAR DEFEAT YOU.

This is very important in everyday life. No matter what the circumstances are—fight through it because the pain is well worth the risk. Without pain there is no appreciation of pleasure. Do not be afraid. It is time to be courageous.

They tell you to think outside the box and to color within the lines, but follow your vision despite what others may think. *GO FOR IT!* Great examples are Steve Jobs and Bob Ross. They did what they believed in. If you don't, it won't exist. Who's to say taking a risk and going against the odds you won't win? **Don't allow fear to stop you.** Fear is an illusion. Go confidently in the direction of your dreams, and dream big.

Not one person on earth became successful by being too fearful to keep trying to reach their goal.

PUT YOUR GAME FACE ON.

No matter how tired and beat down you are you cannot be content with being tired and beat down! We all have weak moments. Stand up for yourself, what you believe in, and give it your all. Don't let other people convince you you're not good enough. **Push through it**. You will feel so much better about yourself once you conquer that feeling of stepping outside of your comfort zone. No matter how weak you are, scared you are, or how close you are to losing a battle, you cannot—I repeat, you cannot—let them think, not even for a second, that they're defeating you because once they think they are... they already have.

"My attitude is that, if you push me toward something you think is a weakness, then I will turn that perceived weakness into a strength."

Michael Jordan

STICK WITH WHATEVER SUITS YOU BEST.

Variety is good, but you don't always have to switch things up to keep them interesting. Focus on the very things that feed your soul and build you higher.

"The work you do while you procrastinate is probably the work you should be doing for the rest of you life"
- Jessica Hische

Devote your time to one goal, and you'll succeed beyond your limitations.

Envision.
Aim.
Execute.
Set a higher level of achievement.
Repeat.

LOVE IS A CHOICE.

No matter what, obstacles come and go. The two of you together can defeat anything that tries to ruin your relationship. Love is about being able to confide in one another; finding comfort in your partner because they love, respect, and accept who you are.

FOR INSTANCE:

I will never spill the beans because your trust in me is more important than being mad at you for 15 minutes. It's all about our communication and commitment that keeps our thoughts sane and us together, as long as we're on the same page. It's not just about being my significant other, it's about being my best friend and not judging me or leaving me for making a couple of mistakes. Love is knowing that nothing in this world can make us or break us but you and I. It's growing up and old together and not feeling like we are missing anything because what we have together is way more than we'll have ever alone anyway.

GO WITH THE FLOW.
DON'T TRY TO FORCE
ANYTHING. EVERYTHING
THAT IS MEANT TO BE
WILL HAPPEN
NATURALLY.
PEOPLE ARE GOING TO DO
WHAT THEY WANT
REGARDLESS.
YOU CAN'T STOP THEM
NO MATTER HOW HARD
YOU TRY. YOU CAN ONLY
HOPE THAT BY PROVIDING
THEM WITH LOVE,
LOYALTY, AND RESPECT
THEY'LL GIVE YOU THE
SAME IN RETURN.
IF NOT, DON'T SWEAT IT.
LET THEM GO.

PEOPLE FROM YOUR PAST MAY HAVE CREATED A FALSE IMAGE OF YOU.

They might even try to influence others to continue this image they wrongly portray of you. Instead of them taking the time to realize your self-growth, they'll continue to spread hatred and slander. Show these people a new and improved you. **YOUR ACTIONS WILL ALWAYS SPEAK LOUDER.** Keep your chin held high and hold your composure. We've all played the villain or victim role in our lives. We can learn from our mistakes and make changes, or we can continue down the same path. It's a choice we have to make. If they choose to keep the past a part of the present, then maybe they should no longer be invited to your future.

KEEP IN MIND: PEOPLE FEED OFF OF ONE ANOTHER'S ENERGY LIKE A CHAIN REACTION. WITH A BETTER YOU COMES A BETTER ME.

Take criticism and allow it to bring you growth, not anger.

Not everyone is going to understand or accept you for you, but take the time to try and teach them.

Those who have the most anger are in need of the most love. Show them there's hope and be someone to believe in.

Instead of pointing fingers, grab and hold someone's hand. We are all in need of one another in one way or another.

Don't be a negative Nancy.
(Sorry, Nancy)
Be a positive Peter.
Shed light.

FAMILY is everything, even if you can't stand each other sometimes. When push comes to shove, it's family who should have your back. It's family who should show you unconditional love and support. It's family who should matter most.

Family doesn't necessarily have to mean those related by blood. They're the people in your life you choose to become and stay apart of.

FAMILY IS TRUST.
FAMILY IS LOYALTY.
FAMILY IS RESPECT.

FAMILY IS LOVE.

Create the one you desire.

ALL HUMANS CRAVE LOVE.

We all want someone who will inspire us and love us until our time is done. When was the last time you looked at someone selflessly and genuinely cared about his or her happiness? When was the last time you wanted to love somebody without trying to change who they are? When was the last time you went out of your way to do something nice without expecting anything back in return?

> *We don't love properly. We love selfishly.*
> *That's the problem.*

Love is not just about you. Love is not just about me.
Love is about us.

Love is about making each other happy. Go out of your way for the one you love simply because it will put a smile on their face. There is nothing better than giving, or receiving love. Nothing. And if they love you, they'll make it about you too. That's how love balances out: when you BOTH love each other enough to do whatever it takes to make and keep each other happy.

"I was never really insane except upon occasions when my heart was touched."
— Edgar Allan Poe

FLASHLIGHTS...

There are certain people you cross paths with that you'll always remember. No matter what has happened between the two of you, these are the important people who have taught you something pure, something inspirational and something life changing. These are your teachers, your leaders, and your most valuable effective human beings. They're the type of people who come into your life with a flashlight when you're in the dark and help you shine your light. Even if these people come and go, they'll still shine to you and manage to outshine a lot of people. Their aura rubs off on you. No time is wasted because you gain wisdom, knowledge and power from the time you share with one another. Cherish the people who spark your soul. They're golden. They invest in you and take the time to show you something refreshing and genuine: that is something to be carried with you for the rest of your life. It is now your turn to be the teacher. Encourage, inspire and motivate others to do more, see more and be more in life. Start using what you have to help others. No matter how small you think it is. Nothing is too small; even a bunch of snowflakes can cause a severe snowstorm. No matter how insignificant it may seem, every little bit counts.

Melissa Molomo

51

Some of the things that hurt us actually heal us. Some of the things that confuse us actually give us the answer. Sometimes rejection is redirection to something better.

GOD IS WORKING. TRUST HIM AND BE THANKFUL.

YOU ARE WHERE YOU ARE FOR A REASON.

YOUR ENEMIES ARE ALWAYS WAITING FOR YOU TO SLIP UP. BE CAREFUL. STAY BALANCED.

Fame is the American Dream, but once you get it, it could be your worst nightmare. You really have to be one of the strong, unbreakable ones to handle this kind of lifestyle. Yes, as we are all aware, there are a lot of great perks to being famous: the stardom, the money, the travelling, doing what you love, etc. However, what people don't seem to realize is how damaging it can be. They see the glamorous part of it, what the sources claim it to be, but what they don't see is what really goes on behind the scenes. By all means, your favorite artist might make a great musician, but not be your favorite human being.

What if we looked at our favorite celebrities for the human beings they are? Sometimes society is quick to judge. People are always looking for a way to bring you down.

We are all noticed in one way, shape or form, but imagine being put under a microscope for your every move to be magnified. Imagine being criticized for every little thing you do, and not having a moment of privacy even when it's time for a bathroom break. Imagine having a child and getting trampled or followed to your house by paparazzi.

This is the "price of fame," but what is the price of humble humanity? The world needs more genuinely good people.

All I can say is famous or not, I hope the corrupted people and this industry never get the best of you and that you always stay true to who you are. Negative people love to stop something positive. God is love and you were born to shine. Good for you!

I hope you only surround yourself with people who want the best for you, and that you never work so hard that you begin to lose sight of what really matters.

NO IS NOT THE ANSWER.

SOMETIMES YOU HAVE TO PUT YOUR FOOT DOWN. BE A LITTLE MORE STERN AND NOT LET PEOPLE MISTAKE YOUR SWEETNESS FOR WEAKNESS.

YOU WANT SOMETHING?

YOU HAVE TO BE DETERMINED ENOUGH TO GO GET IT.

THERE IS NO LOVE, LIFE OR HAPPINESS IN FEAR.

ZIP.
ZERO.

IF SOMEONE DOESN'T WANT TO BE A PART OF YOUR LIFE, WHY WOULD YOU BEG THEM TO STAY?

Don't allow someone to take advantage of you. If they don't see the good in your heart, allow yourself to let them go.

Someone who wants to be part of your life will be. It's really as simple as it sounds. Try your best to be the bigger person and never allow your last words to be negative.

Once a person notices you are no longer in reach, they tend to realize your unavailability and reconsider wanting you in their life. When the ball is in your court, assume home court advantage. Don't cause a turnover and give your opponent the ball too easily. Make them work for it.

Melissa Molomo

AN APOLOGY IS NOT AN ERASER TO PAIN. IT'S MORE LIKE WHITE OUT!

Our job here on earth is to love—not to corrupt. Although we are humanly flawed, sinful and made of mistakes, we must try to right our wrongs by clothing ourselves with compassion, kindness and love everyday…not just when we're in the mood to be fashionable.

BUILD YOUR CREDIT. PROPERLY.

Credit card debt is an uncomfortable situation. I've witnessed this too many times for my liking from people I loved so dearly. So I don't want you (if you haven't already) or your child to make the same mistakes.

Do not take on more than you can handle.

Always try to have double the amount, this way you have something to fall back on—just in case.

Don't dig and bury yourself in a hole you can't get yourself out of.

You'll live the rest of your life miserable and in debt.

DO NOT FORCE OR RUSH LOVE.
ALLOW LOVE TO DEVELOP ON
ITS OWN TIME. JUST BECAUSE
YOU MAY BE INFATUATED WITH
SOMEONE DOESN'T NECESSARILY
MEAN THIS IS THE PERSON YOU
ARE MEANT TO BE WITH. THE
FIRST BOND YOU WANT TO BUILD
WITH SOMEONE IS A FRIENDSHIP.
FOCUS ON LEARNING ABOUT ONE
ANOTHER AND UNDERSTAND
WHO THIS PERSON TRULY IS. DO
NOT GO BY THE IMAGES YOU
CREATE IN YOUR HEAD OF WHO
THIS PERSON CAN POTENTIALLY
BE. IF YOU ACCEPT ONE AN
OTHER FOR WHO YOU TRULY
ARE, YOU WON'T HAVE TO DEAL
WITH THE DISAPPOINTMENTS OF
EXPECTATIONS THAT YOU SET
FOR ONE ANOTHER LATER ON.

A LETTER TO MY QUEENS:

It is time to become a woman who isn't going to allow a man to constantly walk all over her all because "she loves him." It is time to become a woman who knows her worth and what she is capable of. It is time to become a woman who knows she can surpass any limitations any one sets for her, because she believes in herself. It is time to become a woman who is well aware of her independence. It is time to become a woman who has enough **self-respect** to walk away from a man who tries to convince her to think any less of herself. It is time to become the type of woman who knows her worth at all times, even during her weakest moments. It is time...

No woman should settle for less than she deserves. No woman should operate strictly on a man's watch, but learn to do things on her own time.

Have enough strength to walk away when you know in your heart it's time for change. It is time to become the woman you were born to be... a Queen.

No woman should value a man so much that she forgets her worth.

The time is now.
TICK. TOCK.

61

WHEN THERE ARE SIGNS IN FRONT OF YOUR FACE REPEATEDLY SHOWING YOU SOMETHING ISN'T RIGHT FOR YOU, IT'S PROBABLY BECAUSE SOMETHING SERIOUSLY ISN'T RIGHT FOR YOU. STOP AVOIDING THE SIGNS AND STOP TRYING TO FORCE A PIECE OF A PUZZLE THAT CLEARLY DOES NOT FIT, WALK AWAY—ALTHOUGH IT MIGHT BE YOUR HARDEST CHOICE, IT WILL BE YOUR HEALTHIEST.

I DON'T KNOW ABOUT YOU, BUT I NEED STABILITY IN A RELATIONSHIP.

Not one that flip-flops where it's **"I love you"** today and **"I hate you"** tomorrow. I think people in these kinds of relationships need to stop playing the villain and victim role and realize they're in it together. Learn to accept the possibility that the person you're with is not the enemy, and stop treating them as if they are. Take good care of those you love and who love you in return—that way you both can keep it consistent. **Let's be real here, you're probably not the easiest person to handle, so I suggest you stop taking your past out on your present because that is only going to mess up your future.**

Give yourself a chance to fully love again. Not cold-heartedly.

REALIZE WHAT YOU HAVE WHILE YOU HAVE IT; SO IF YOU LOSE IT, YOU WON'T HAVE TO DEAL WITH THE REPERCUSSIONS OF NOT DOING WHAT YOU WERE SUPPOSED TO BE DOING.

TRY NOT TO BE SO HARD ON YOURSELF, ESPECIALLY IN CHALLENGING MOMENTS.

You are growing and educating yourself through times when you may not feel comfortable. Give yourself some credit for stepping out of your comfort zone because not everyone is going to give you the credit you deserve.

As long as your heart is pure, your sins will be forgiven. Pray for redemption. Don't worry about who you aren't—be happy with who you are. The first step of progression is realizing you are a sinner in order to realize that you'll do much better in life trying to be like a saint.

"The ultimate measure of a man is not where he stands in moments of comfort and convenience, but where he stands at times of challenge and controversy."
Martin Luther King, Jr.

UNTIL YOU ARE FULLY BROKEN, YOU DON'T KNOW WHAT YOU ARE MADE OF. BEING BROKEN GIVES YOU THE ABILITY TO BUILD YOURSELF ALL OVER AGAIN. THIS TIME AROUND, REBUILD YOURSELF STRONGER THAN EVER.

LISTEN...

I know what it's like to feel borderline broken and defeated. I catch myself becoming a little more moody than usual. I shut down quicker because I don't always feel the need to explain myself. It becomes hard for me to fake a smile and pretend like everything is all right. However, that's the thing—while I'm being judged every single day, I know me. I know me better than anyone, and even though I've fallen, I will rise again, stronger than before. I've been broken hearted. I've been poor, discouraged, and betrayed but it's never stopped me. The opportunity to rebuild myself was hard at first, but refreshing in the end. It made me who I am. I know what I've been through, and I know what I can get through. No matter how lost or defeated I am, **I WILL NEVER LOSE.**

LAZINESS IS A CURSE.

Every single one of us has the ability to succeed in life, but so many of us choose to go a different route. A lot of us choose to allow our laziness to defeat our determination instead.

Lying in our beds for a few hours, especially when we're down, seems relaxing and peaceful, but there are some serious side effects. Yes, sleep may recharge your battery, but sleeping too much will drain you physically, mentally and emotionally. You'll actually find yourself feeling worthless and depressed because you don't have much going on. The hardest part about this is once you feel worthless, all your motivation is gone and it's not something you can easily get back.

If you have this issue, NOW is the time to force yourself to get up and unbind that unhealthy spell of laziness. Otherwise, you will allow days, weeks, and even months pass you by. Literally force yourself by always planning a busy day. In order to succeed in life, you have to be able to wake up! Begin the day with a positive outlook. If not, you'll find yourself loving sleep more than you love success, life and love. What's the point of that? Every single one of us is worth something special. Every single one of us is brilliant in our own special way. Find out what it is.

YOU CREATE THE LIFE YOU CHOOSE TO LIVE, SO GET OUT THERE AND SHOW THE WORLD A LIFE WORTH WAKING UP FOR.

"A life of leisure and a life of laziness are two things. There will be sleeping enough in the grave."

-Benjamin Franklin

TRY NOT TO LOSE YOUR FAITH IN OTHERS DUE TO A FEW CORRUPT SOULS.

There will always be rotten apples in the bunch, but that does not mean you have to become one. *Stay ripe*. Kindness kills negativity. Instead of giving someone a dirty look or a dry response, give a genuine smile. Instead of reacting right away and jumping down someone's throat, keep it calm, cool and collected. Your reaction will throw them off, but in a positive way.

Learn to communicate without throwing verbal jabs.

Our main problem when we get ourselves into confrontation is to say really harmful things. Don't look to hurt. Look to heal. You can't expect jabs to be thrown without someone feeling the need to retaliate.

"Better to remain silent and be thought a fool than to speak out and remove all doubt."

-Abraham Lincoln

EVERYONE YOU MEET IN LIFE IS BETTER THAN YOU AT SOMETHING.

Everyone has his or her own special niche. Be humble enough to learn from them.

The person you may be talking down to, brushing off or criticizing is more valuable than you are aware of.

NOT EVERYONE YOU MEET IN LIFE IS GOING TO KISS YOUR ASS AND TAKE YOUR CRAP.

Pay attention to how you treat people and what you say to them, especially when you're stressed, or you might end up losing out on someone great.

People ask what the difference is between a boss and a leader. A boss only cares about authority: you do this; you do that. A leader's focus is influence: I'll help do this; I'll help do that.

BE A LEADER!

TRY NOT TO ASSUME, ACCUSE, JUDGE OR CRITICIZE.

We cannot be so quick to point fingers and jump the gun if we are not able to admit our own faults. Just because someone does not know, does not mean YOU DON'T!

Where is that guilty conscience of yours hiding? You aren't being hypocritical now, are you? Just because you haven't been caught, does not mean you're not guilty!

Be real. Apologize. Admit your faults and move forward. Don't request someone's eye, when it is yours that should be missing.

> **"It's when you hide things that you choke on them."**
> **-Charles Bukowski**

LIKE IT OR NOT!

You are being judged based upon your surroundings. As I've been saying *when you surround yourself with people who are successful, you are most likely to be successful yourself.* When you surround yourself with partygoers, you are most likely going to spend your time partying and not worrying about priorities as much as you should. It's cool to have fun, but you can either learn and grow or mess up and back track from the people you have in your life keeping you focused. Look at the 5 people you spend the most of your time with: What are they like? What do they do? How do they treat people? How do they operate? Are they successful? Are they on the right track?

I know what it's like to care about people, but not everyone you meet in life is meant to stay a part of your life.

You don't always have to be serious, but know when it's time to get serious.

Melissa Molomo

BUTTERFLY EFFECT...

Who would have thought the people who caused you the most harm wouldn't matter years down the road? There's no more sense of heartache, pain, revenge—not even an ounce worth of bitterness toward them. Not anymore. Who would've thought the people you never thought you'd be able to get over no longer exist in your life? They were there once upon a time. You may have even loved them so much that it hurt to know they were the ones who initially caused a butterfly effect in your life.

All it takes is for one person to come and make a few minor changes in certain major circumstances to cause a large change in outcome for the rest of your life. This person, unfortunately, happened to cause a lot of traumatizing events. Not saying it was intentional, but it's just what happened. Once you finally got rid of them, the pain started to heal.

Who would've thought you'd be able to see them out years from now with a smile on your face. Even though you two no longer know each other it's good to see that person smiling, not even acknowledging the bumpy past exists. Pretending like they don't know... You're smiling too.

SOMEDAY, SOMEBODY'S GOING TO LOOK AT YOU AND REALIZE WHY IT NEVER WORKED OUT WITH ANYONE ELSE. I UNDERSTAND THE HEARTACHE AND PAIN YOU'RE FEELING RIGHT NOW BECAUSE I'VE FELT IT BEFORE—EVERYONE HAS. I KNOW IT SUCKS, BUT YOUR HEART WILL MEND. THERE'S SOMEONE OUT THERE WHO WILL LOVE YOU AND ACCEPT YOU ENOUGH THAT THEY MIGHT EVEN MAKE YOU FORGET YOUR HEART WAS BROKEN TO BEGIN WITH. EVEN IF YOU DON'T THINK YOU'LL EVER LOVE AGAIN, YOU WILL. DON'T STAND IDLE. MOVE AND BE GUIDED. FALL IN LOVE EVERY DAY—NOT JUST WITH HUMAN BEINGS, BUT WITH MOMENTS, MUSIC, WRITINGS, NATURE...WHATEVER SOOTHES YOU.

What are you content with?

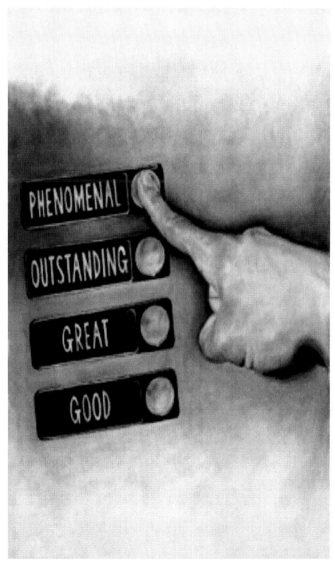

ALWAYS ACCEPT YOURSELF FOR WHO YOU ARE, WHILE KNOWING YOU CAN STILL WORK ON BETTERING YOURSELF.

WOMEN CAN MAKE IT HARDER FOR MEN TO CHEAT...

If only they would just respect themselves and each other. Yes, it takes two to tango, but women have more willpower and can fight temptation better than men. It's not an excuse. It's in our nature. We were put on this earth as nurturers, but we must realize no one can value us until we value ourselves. It is our actions that teach people how to treat us. We decide what is acceptable and what is unacceptable.

I will take a stand for the good women of the world and ask you to learn to love yourself enough to honor your body and not give it away to anybody just because they gave you a bit of time, attention and/or effort. I ask you to respect other women and know they are not the enemy. There is no need for ulterior motives. You may not see your worth just yet, you may even be content with the way you are, but I want you to know you are worth way more than you present yourself to be.

Ask yourself: how are you a prize if anyone who approaches you can win you? Be a woman of dignity, power and respect. You'll see a huge difference in not only the person you become but also in the people you attract.

Melissa Molomo

**IF YOU WANT TO BE
TREATED LIKE
A LADY
YOU CAN'T JUST ACT
LIKE ONE—YOU
ACTUALLY HAVE TO BE
ONE.**

**SELF-RESPECT IS BY FAR
THE MOST ATTRACTIVE
TRAIT A WOMAN CAN
HAVE. FOLLOWED BY
INDEPENDENCE—BUT
NOT SO MUCH OF IT
THAT SHE CAN'T RELY
ON HER MAN FOR
ANYTHING.**

SINGLE AND WONDERING WHY? MAYBE IT'S NOT YOU. MAYBE IT'S WHAT YOU'RE ATTRACTED TO.

As humans, we become attached and dependent on those we truly care about. Then, if they decide to leave one day, it seems like our whole world comes crashing down. We lose hope. We become miserable. We even convince ourselves that we've hit rock bottom. Sometimes it takes months to move on and recover, even years. We tend to convince ourselves that even though there are plenty of fish in the sea, that there is only one fish that is going to fulfill us. Let me start off by saying, LOVE is great and two can be better than one, but when there is only one person doing all the loving, the one still holding on must finally learn to let go. This time around, we must break the cycle and learn to be completely content; we must learn to find happiness within ourselves and not count on someone to be our happiness. The individuals we enter into relationships with should ADD value to who we are and how we are. We can't become traumatized by every failed relationship. When we break, we rebuild—ideally, this time for the better.

Melissa Molomo

STOP COMPARING YOURSELF TO OTHER PEOPLE. YOU'RE ONE OF A KIND.

Be yourself, but choose to be your kind self.
Have courage. Inspire, motivate and trust to not
only have hope in yourself, but to be able to place
hope within the lives of others—without placing
harm. Never let fear get in the way of doing what
you love and being with those you love.

THERE IS NO TOMORROW.
BE WHAT YOU LOVE.
SAY WHAT YOU LOVE.
DO WHAT YOU LOVE.
&
LOVE WHAT YOU LOVE.

Don't leave earth being a coward. Go out with a
bang. Your chance tonight may be gone
tomorrow. Take the opportunity while you have
it and run free.

LIVE AND LOVE.
MATTER OF FACT,
LIVE IN LOVE.

SURVIVE.

GROW.

EVOLVE.

When it comes to everlasting love, it is most important to not give up especially when things get rough. We are given so many obstacles, at times it may seem that we'll never overcome them. There is constant annoyance, bickering and little jabs thrown here or there, but as long as there's a common understanding of, "I love you" and "you love me," I will not do anything to jeopardize what I have with you. I will not—no matter how much I can't stand you—go behind your back and run into another person's arms. At the end of the day, someone who loves you is not going anywhere— no ifs, no ands, no buts.

I MAY NOT BE ABLE TO SPOIL YOU WITH EXPENSIVE GIFTS, BUT I'LL SPOIL YOU WITH LOYALTY AND MAKE YOU FEEL RICH.

THE WORLD IS FILLED
WITH A BUNCH OF PEOPLE
WALKING DEAD. BRING
SOMEONE BACK TO LIFE.
THEY COULD BE COLD,
CORRUPT, SELFISH—EVEN
BROKEN-HEARTED, BUT
WITH YOUR PATIENCE,
UNDERSTANDING,
KINDNESS AND
UNCONDITIONAL LOVE, YOU
CAN MEND THEM.
AS LONG AS THEY ARE
WILLING TO LEARN, BE
COURAGEOUS ENOUGH TO
TEACH THEM WHAT IT'S
LIKE TO BE ALIVE AND TO
LIVE AGAIN.

IF YOU'RE NOT OVER YOUR EX...

And what has happened to you in the past, do not jump into another relationship so quickly. You are entitled to your healing process. You shouldn't put all of your weight on someone's shoulders and expect them to speed up the process. Get rid of your baggage. If you find yourself taking everything that your **EX** did to you out on your new partner, you need to be a little more considerate. Realize they do not deserve that. No one does.

Take the time to heal yourself before you jump into something again. *Don't sleep with someone to get over someone else. We all have the tendency to jump into something when we are broken hearted.* Don't end up playing yourself by trying to play someone else. Take it slow. Be honest. *Don't do what was done to you to someone else.*

Have a heart.

IF SOMEONE WANTS TO BE WITH YOU—THEY WILL BE WITH YOU.

IF SOMEONE WANTS TO TALK TO YOU—THEY WILL CALL YOU.

IF SOMEONE WANTS TO SEE YOU—THEY WILL MAKE TIME FOR YOU.

The whole guessing game thing is getting a little old. You want to be with someone? Take the risk, and tell them. You want something real? Offer something real.

BROKEN CANNOT FIX BROKEN.

Our thoughts are powerful. The ways we think develop our reactions, but our reactions aren't always the result of the power in our thoughts. Some thinking doesn't occur until after the damage of a reaction is done.

We have to get better at this.

If you are broken, focus on rebuilding yourself before you try to fix someone who is also broken. Your intentions may be pure, but you may be causing more damage than you realize—not only to yourself, but to the person you are with.

FIX YOU FIRST.

FOLLOW THESE GUIDELINES:
"No, thank you.
I'll pass."

Who said you have to wake up every single morning at 7:00 on the dot and go to a job you absolutely hate in order to be successful? Who said making a couple of bucks for doing hours worth of work is equivalent to more than what you are paid to do is the recipe for achievement? Not me. Slavery still exists. You don't have to settle for a miserable or basic life, if that is not the life you want to live. Remain passionate, be creative and exercise patience. Persistence is the key to unlock any door that leads to success. Do not settle because "that's how life works," or because that is what people expect you to do since it is what they've always done. Yes, income is necessary to survive, but not at the act of forfeiting your passion and investing all of your time into working a job you don't enjoy.

You have a dream? Turn it into reality—no matter how many demons you have to face to make it happen. You can make it happen.

Don't set guidelines, set deadlines. Get it done.

> **"Logic will get you from A to Z;**
> **imagination will get you everywhere."**
> **—Albert Einstein**

TRUE HAPPINESS NEVER EXISTED FOR ANYONE WHO SETTLED FOR LESS THAN THEY'VE IMAGINED.

THE PROBLEM -__-

The problem with this world is that people are too selfish when it comes to success that it somehow, someway always has to be about them. Why? Why not help pull somebody up the ladder instead of pushing him or her off of it? There are a lot of snakes out there. Be aware of the wolves in sheep's clothing. They are cutthroat because they compete for anything and everything they've got. They don't want the spotlight to be taken from them, but in reality, what they don't notice is that it's not about the spotlight. It's about changing lives for the better, doing God's work. It's about giving people something new to learn and something to improve on. Giving people something/someone to believe in is one of the greatest gifts. It will make them feel as if they're not alone. Inspire the people you come in contact with, and make a difference by being a part of someone's life.

I would give people the food off my plate. I couldn't eat while watching you starve. Maybe that's why I'll never be insanely rich because I'm too worried about everyone else around me being good.

Give a helping hand instead of a tripping foot.

"If you enter this world knowing you are loved and you leave this world knowing the same, then everything that happens in between can be dealt with."

Michael Jackson

GIVE YOURSELF SOME CREDIT:

No one on earth has lived life in your shoes. No one has seen, heard or witnessed everything you have been through, but you. No one on earth is you, but you. And that's what makes you a masterpiece. Do not cloud your vision by trying to be like someone else. Do not change your mind due to the thoughts of someone else. You are doing a great job at being you. Always stay true to yourself and have the audacity to remain **BeYOU**tiful.

"Today you are You, that is truer than true. There is no one alive who is Youer than You."

Dr. Seuss

THE ONLY WAY YOU FAIL IS IF YOU QUIT.

YOU WEREN'T BORN TO BE A QUITTER, SO DON'T EVEN THINK ABOUT LEAVING THIS EARTH AS ONE.

TRY. TRY. TRY AGAIN.

THINKING TOO MUCH WILL PLANT FALSE IMAGES IN YOUR HEAD.

Train your brain to get rid of the roots before they end up growing a huge habit in your garden.

Your painful thoughts are your inner demons. Tell them to flee, before they even think about getting comfortable.

Trust me, negative thoughts will mentally drain you.

Think good thoughts. If it is easier said than done, you have to stop making excuses for yourself.

Your mind has to learn to be healthy. Train the brain like you would train your muscles.

Pushhhhhh yourself.

JUST BECAUSE YOU ARE MAD AT SOMEBODY TODAY, DOES NOT MEAN YOU CAN'T BE HAPPY WITH THEM TOMORROW.

Words can be extremely dangerous so we should all learn to speak with severe caution. Now If I were to type as carelessly as some people tend to speak, you wouldn't be able to read what I'm writing. *That's why writing is so powerful, not only because you can think before you speak, but you can take the time to edit, delete and rewrite before you put it out there for the world to see.* The words that come out of your mouth—you can never take back.

If you have an issue with somebody, address it politely, instead of making matters worse. Don't turn to someone else, turn to the person you have the "problem" with. Nobody else is going to fix your problems for you. Most of the time, they only make things worse.

Through the miscommunication of words, our ideas tend to get mixed up in other peoples' heads. Soon after, you'll catch yourself in the "he said, she said" category of words you may not have even said. Always remember: there are two sides to every story, but don't neglect to take into consideration that your story may be based on miscommunication.

Take matters into your own hands, be mature enough to communicate your feelings properly. It only takes one person to be the bigger person. No longer hesitate; be that person. You'll sleep better at night being at peace with yourself.

96

SOMEONE WHO ONLY GREW UP UNDERSTANDING ENGLISH CANNOT COMPREHEND SPANISH UNLESS IT IS SOMETHING THEY ARE TAUGHT—

THE SAME THING GOES FOR LOVE.

YOU CANNOT HOLD ONTO SOMEBODY WHO DOES NOT WANT TO BE HELD.

It is better to be alone and lonely than it is to be with the wrong person. You are not giving the right person an opportunity to come in that way. The only thing you two are doing is cheating yourselves out of true love. Do not waste another day, month or year on someone you're not in love with due to *comfort*.

Step out of your comfort zone before you get stuck and end up staying there.

If you want me in your life, put me there and keep me there. I shouldn't have to fight for a spot. Love is not a competition, and entering into a relationship that's otherwise is something I'm just not willing to put my heart through. It's simple. If you want me in your life, love me. If you don't, let me be.

DESPITE WHATEVER'S BEEN GOING ON IN YOUR LIFE, I WANT YOU TO KNOW HOW SPECIAL YOU ARE.

I think we all get caught up in such nonsense that we tend to forget to give credit when credit is due. I need you to know you are appreciated beyond belief, even if you don't always feel that way. I want you to know that you are loved to the moon and back, flaws and all.

You are an amazing, intelligent, beautiful soul—just the way God intended you to be.

Don't ever forget that.

People take their loved ones for granted every day, but somehow, someway, sooner or later, reality hits them. And when it does, they realize that the person they constantly took advantage of is no longer in reach, no longer jumping over hurdles, no longer going above and beyond and no longer putting up with their baggage. They weren't playing their part as a significant other because they were too busy playing games—all the while forgetting you were the ultimate prize to be won. Everything was one sided. Then suddenly, out of nowhere, there was no more waiting for your calls, your texts or to be treated properly. Instead, the tables turned…

Well, well, well, who would've thought? The person you never thought would leave you even after all you've done and gotten away with finally had enough strength and courage in them to say goodbye. When in reality, this was the one person who actually had enough strength and courage in them to love you, but your non-existent efforts to make things better took a toll and paid the price.

NOBODY WANTS TO BE SOMEBODY'S PUNCHING BAG.

Nobody wants to be somebody's doormat. Nobody wants to feel unloved by the one person they love the most.

Who would have thought, out of the blue… it's now you doing all the waiting.

Be careful. If this isn't already—it could be you.

Don't be a little too late.

Don't get flat lined by the one person you love because you weren't playing your part. Other people will always audition for your role, so maintain it.

Someone you take for granted is someone another will appreciate.

Don't lose your opportunity.

LETTING GO OF CERTAIN PEOPLE IS NOT SAYING, "I HATE YOU," IT'S SAYING, "I LOVE ME MORE."

Sometimes you have to let go of certain people for a little while to make them realize what they're missing when you're gone.

Give them time to learn how to appreciate you. If they don't, at least you'll know you made the right decision.

Be careful of who you decide to spend your time with because not everybody cares about wasting your time. Every moment counts. Your friends are the people you pick and choose to be with— just make sure you know the true definition of friendship. Pick the ones who better you, who want you to succeed, who teach you things, who are not only there for the good times but through the bad times, too. Pick the ones who don't get you into trouble but keep you out of trouble. Pick wisely because your friends are a reflection of you.

YOU CAN NEVER CHANGE SOMEBODY'S PAST, BUT YOU CAN HELP THEM BUILD A BIGGER, BETTER AND BRIGHTER FUTURE.

DON'T HESITATE TO ASK FOR HELP.

The more brains involved, the smarter the project becomes. Steal ideas from anyone who sparks inspiration in your brain to be great—the greatest ideas are borrowed, copied or stolen anyway.

Choose whatever you'd want to leave out or add in to make them even better. Combine your imaginations. Creativity is at its best when you know nothing is completely original anymore.

When you say "I wish"—it's like saying something is impossible and would take a miracle to happen. Instead, start saying, "I will". You are blessed to be alive and able to say it.

Make smarter decisions. Reach for the stars. Those who say, "I can't" lack ambition. If you want to generate a different crowd of people, ask them what they think you're lacking.

NOTHING IS MORE ATTRACTIVE THAN A MAN WHO IS FULLY COMMITTED TO HIS WOMAN. NO MATTER HOW MANY FEMALES ARE DRAWN TO HIM, HIS EYES, EARS AND HANDS ALWAYS REMAIN ON HIS WOMAN.

(And vice versa)

I don't care if you've been in a relationship for one week, seven months or fifteen years, you should never stop trying to impress one another.

Don't become too lazy or be too comfortable, do something your loved one will thank you for.

TRUTHFUL CRITICISM COULD BE THE MISSING PIECE TO YOUR PUZZLE.

Listen to the opinions of others, and educate yourself. Whatever you are looking to do, take the initiative to learn to do it. Google it, buy books, watch YouTube videos—whatever it takes to improve your knowledge on something. Don't be negative about rejection. The most memorable people are successful failures. Try and try again... Fix it over and over again until it's exactly the way you envisioned it.

Being satisfied is like saying there is no more room for improvement. Keep perfecting. There is always something you can work on.

Whatever ideas you come across, jot them down, so you don't forget what's next on your to do list.

You have to have a goal in order to be able to score.

Melissa Molomo

YOU WON'T EVER HAVE TO WORRY ABOUT BEING BOSSED AROUND WHEN YOU MAKE YOURSELF YOUR OWN BOSS.

LIVE
YOUR
DREAMS

INVESTMENT:

I didn't invest my time for us to fail. I believe in you, and as long as you put in effort to make this work, you can always count on me to be there to meet you halfway. Even if I tend to get lazy or tired, I will never sleep on you—unless we're cuddling of course. I know I can look at you sometimes and say you're not the easiest person to deal with, but I still love and accept you for it, and when I look at myself in the mirror I know I'm no angel either, but it's nice to know you're okay with that.

You're not my opponent, and I'm not yours. I never want you to feel like we're not on the same team. We're in this together—flawed, raised differently, and misunderstood, yet putting everything we have on the table for a real shot at unfailing love. Yes, we have all of society flaunting themselves at the click of a button, but it's still you and me. No matter how angry or upset we can be at one another, the fact still remains: we're a team. We're a team that doesn't embarrass one another at the drop of a dime; a team that allows truth and communication to fix any errors made along the way; a team that knows when everyone else is going left, you—a hundred percent of the time—will have me going right with you. We're a team that knows it's about building, exploring and establishing a life together. There's no greater feeling than knowing someone's got your back, and we've got each other's. Everyone knows that practice makes perfect, so I'll practice every day to make this perfect with you.

WHATEVER KIND OF DAY YOU'RE HAVING...

Whatever kind of things that are bringing you down… I want you to take the time throughout your day to let it all go. I want you to stop doing what you're doing. Stop stressing about everyone and everything that's going on around you. Stop thinking about all the wrong in your life and give yourself a clean slate. Take a deep breath. Everything is going to be okay as long as you believe it will be. I want you to take a moment to go somewhere peaceful and focus on what is right. Focus on the things to be thankful for. Focus on the thoughts of bettering yourself. In this moment you may feel the power of mercy and peace. Allow your love to be multiplied, because having an epiphany of living a life without love is like being on the earth without the sun. Practice the behavior you expect from others. Be the light in your own life. Be the sun to others.

PEOPLE FEAR LOVE MORE THAN THEY PORTRAY, AND CONSQUENTLY LIVE IN LUST.

Walls have been built due to experiences of pain, disappointment, betrayal, unfaithfulness and even uncertainty. As the years went on, those walls have been strengthened to the point that breaking them seems impossible. Yet, love is easy. It's because of us—the fault of humans—that love has become so difficult and so hard to find. Difficulty manifests itself in the games we play, the lies we tell, the manipulations we employ and the deceit we derive. Relationships don't start or last with selfishness in the midst. Two people who work as one are what lead to success in relationships, and they never forget that love is unselfish. It's supposed to be about us—not just you and not just me, and most certainly, not them.

Temptation can be a bitch. Disagreements are always an issue, along with the miscommunication that accompanies it—and did I mention smothering? It is overwhelming when trust doesn't seem to fully exist. Let's not act foolish. We all know you can't make somebody love you, if they don't by their own free will. So, why are we scared of letting go of a person who *doesn't* love us? That right there is what cripples us to this very day. We all know love is not about pretending or putting on a show, but that's the first thing we do—we love to flaunt our relationships, like they're picture perfect. Yet are they…

Why does the thought of love intimidate people? It could be because they're not ready *to* love themselves. Sounds simple, yet very true. Maybe it is because they've been hurt before. Maybe it is because their fear for love would rather make them fall in lust. Well, if you aren't ready for love, don't drag someone along for the joy ride because before you know it, you'll realize this person didn't even like rollercoasters to begin with—not to mention, they get motion sickness quicker than you can blink. Don't you dare do what you don't want done to you, and don't allow yourself to put thoughts in their head that clearly don't exist.

Learn to love authentically instead of simply pretending to. Learn to love without looking to hurt. Learn to love without force. Learn to love without fear. If you aren't ready for a relationship and have a hard time committing to someone else, there is something called being completely honest and doing the "no strings attached" thing, but at the end of the day that still leaves you alone: a loner—with no one to fully love and appreciate you for the person you truly are. Whereas, you're pretty great and you deserve to be loved, even after the bad things you've done in your life and all the shitty things that have been done to you. Maybe, just take this moment to realize life is so much more beautiful once love is involved. Learn to love a little, if not a lot.

Take a deep breath.
Stand your ground gracefully.
Never settle. Never judge.
Never betray.
You trip and fall; get yourself right back up and try again.
Become stronger.
Become wiser.
Make improvements and teach people what you know.
Spread knowledge.
Keep your innocence.
Stay golden. Remain humble.
Never lose sight of hope and peace within yourself.
Respect yourself. Respect others.
Know your worth. Accept people for who they truly are.
Give a helping hand. Expect nothing in return.
Treat everyone you meet kindly. Be a role model.
Stand out. Lead the way if you know where you're headed.
Love as often as possible.
Fill all of your days with laughter, love and good energy.
ALWAYS SAY WHAT'S REAL.
Dare yourself to be the difference in a world where we're taught to be fake.

GEMS:

TRAVEL. See the world. If you can't afford it, find a job that pays for it.

If you want to keep a secret keep it to yourself.

Don't give with a goal of receiving back. There's no goodness in that.

If your words are not speaking volumes— do not hesitate to put yourself on mute.

Be patient. There are too many people in the world willing to love you the way you need to be loved to remain devastated by those who don't.

If you think you're ALWAYS right, you're not.

Never stop showing acts of kindness because you feel underappreciated.

Nobody likes a barking dog, be humble.

They only have the power to ruin your day if you give them the permission to.

You won't catch success hanging out with failure.

Don't build friendships with people that would rather build bonds with your enemies.

What's so beautiful about humanity is no matter how deep our wounds are our scars heal. Now, all we have to do is stop picking the scab.

If it comes from the heart, it can't be wrong.

When you truly love yourself that's when you'll leave behind everyone and everything that's unhealthy for you.

QUESTIONS FROM MY SUPPORTERS:

Q: How do I feel confident and not compare myself to every other girl? I get jealous easily especially with my boyfriend and it automatically crushes my self-esteem.

A: In all honesty, I truly believe we're all self-conscious at times. The way you're feeling is okay. Just know you are special and rare. There is no one out there in this world who is you. You are unique and beautiful all on your own. As hard as that is to believe when our self esteem is low... Own it. Do things that build you up. Take care of YOU. Focus on what you want to be in this world and be it. Sometimes our significant other doesn't always show the support we need, but continue to do whatever makes you happy. You cannot forget about you and the things you'd do on your own time. Do what makes you feel good. Do the work you want to see done. Persist until you succeed. The more you love yourself, the more they'll love you. Stop comparing yourself to people by accepting who you are. Embrace your flaws. I learned to feel confident in myself by not paying attention to what society thinks is beautiful and by being who I think is beautiful.

Q: How do I trust others again?

A: *First:* you have to learn how to trust yourself. Once you know you can trust who you are, you automatically should have a little faith that there are other people out there who think like you. *Second:* you have to acknowledge the betrayals of others. Accept, forgive and move forward.

Q: How do I deal with heartbreak and moving on afterward?

A: Heartbreak is the worst. It's like the one time we finally open ourselves up, become vulnerable and believe we can trust someone ... BAM! We fall right on our bums and it seems like nothing can cheer us up. Well, everyone is different, but from my experience, the best thing I could have done was surround myself with loyal loved ones and people who make me laugh, all while doing what I love. If you love volleyball, go join a volleyball league three nights a week. Stay as busy as possible, so your thoughts don't eat you alive. Stay away from sad love songs and negative people. They'll keep you down in the dumps.

Q: Do you think that current rap/hip-hop music is a bad influence on the impressionable minds of the younger male generation when it comes to relationships with women?

A: For impressionable minds: **absolutely**—but that's why I love Drake so much. He's one of the rappers out who tries to send pure messages through his music. Of course he has his moments, but—his music is real. In my opinion, it doesn't necessarily have to just be within the rap/hip-hop category. A lot of music nowadays, even television shows and social media, influence the wrong things, especially when it comes to relationships with women and a lot of other things like drug use and violence…that's why it's always good to have willpower and a mind of your own.

Q: Chasing your dreams…what do you do when you're stuck between two dream jobs? One is the impossible, but it's all you think, sleep and dream about and the other is possible and you love it, but it's not your main dream job—just something you're good at?

A: Chase your dreams. Who's to say you're not the person to make the impossible possible? Yes, we have to make money in order to survive and pay bills, so if it's not making you any, then you're going to have to break up your time. However, that doesn't have to mean you need to give up on what you truly love to do. I didn't give up. Remember, we only have a Plan B in the event that Plan A fails—and the only way Plan A will fail is if you quit. Don't quit. Anything is attainable. True success is doing what you want to be doing between the time you get up in the morning and go to bed at night.

CONTACT MELISSA MOLOMO:

WEBSITE:
SAYWHATSREAL.NET
TWITTER:
TWITTER.COM/MSSAYWHATSREAL
FACEBOOK:
FACEBOOK.COM/SAYWHATSREAL
INSTAGRAM:
INSTAGRAM.COM/MISSSAYWHATSREAL

Credits:

Creative Direction and Input:
Kevin Schnurr & JP Meringolo

Editors:
Leslie Salerno, Jesadies Budden, JP Meringolo, Dominiek
Van Dijk

Illustrator:
Lebaron Murray

Inspiration:
God & Humanity

Artwork Contact:
Lebaron Murray
Instagram: @artbyassociation
Lebaron.murray@gmail.com

I hope you enjoyed reading Say What's Real.
Thank you for your loyalty and support.
You are greatly appreciated.
- MM